HELLO DEAR FRIEND!

THANK YOU FOR YOUR SUPPORT AND WELCOME
TO THIS INVITING SPACE THAT WE HAVE CREATED FOR YOU.
WE HOPE YOU WILL FIND FLOW AND MOMENTS OF SERENITY
AS YOU USE AND CREATE WONDERFUL ART
WITH OUR PRINT AND PATTERN PAPER.

by

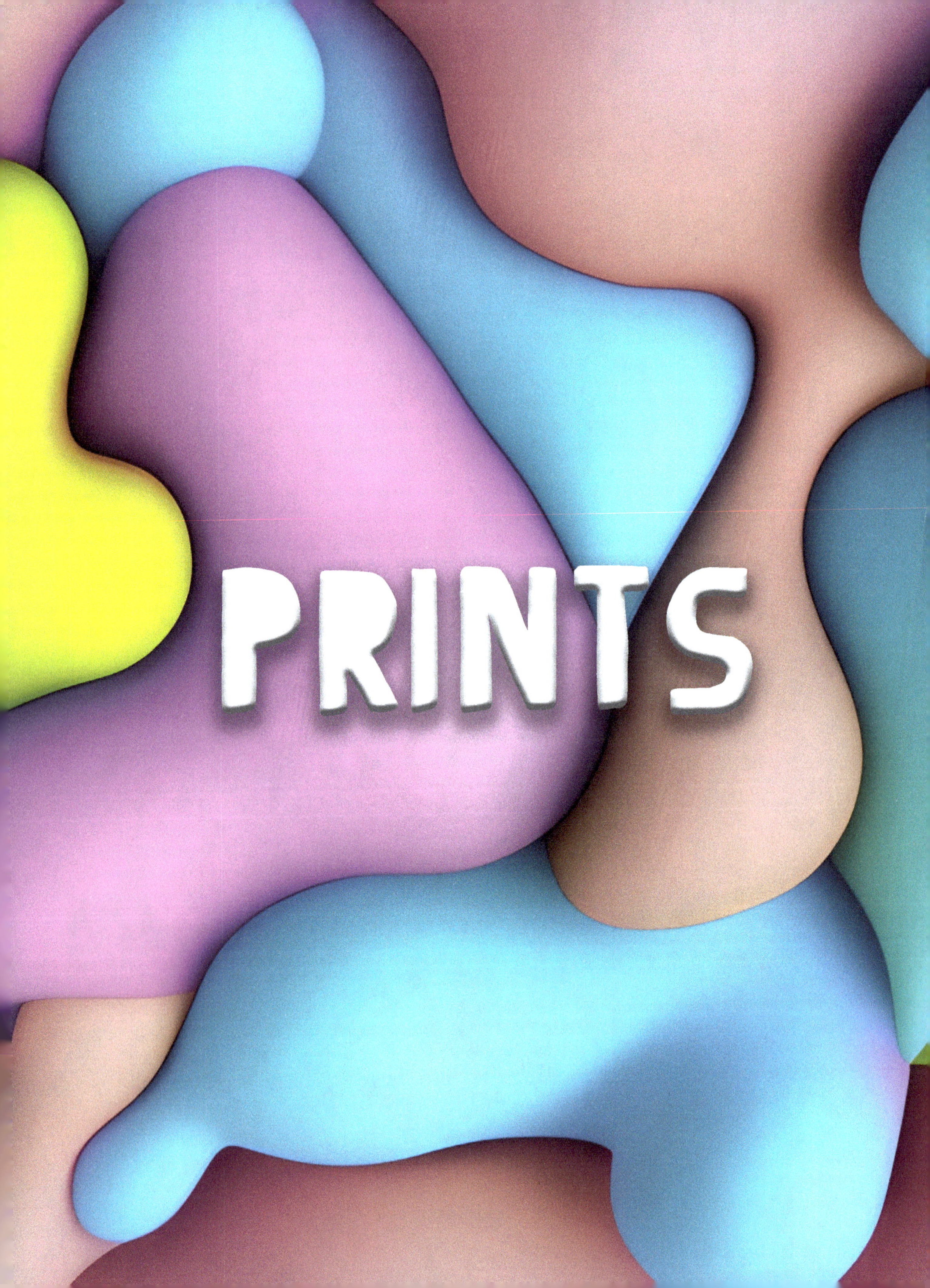
PRINTS

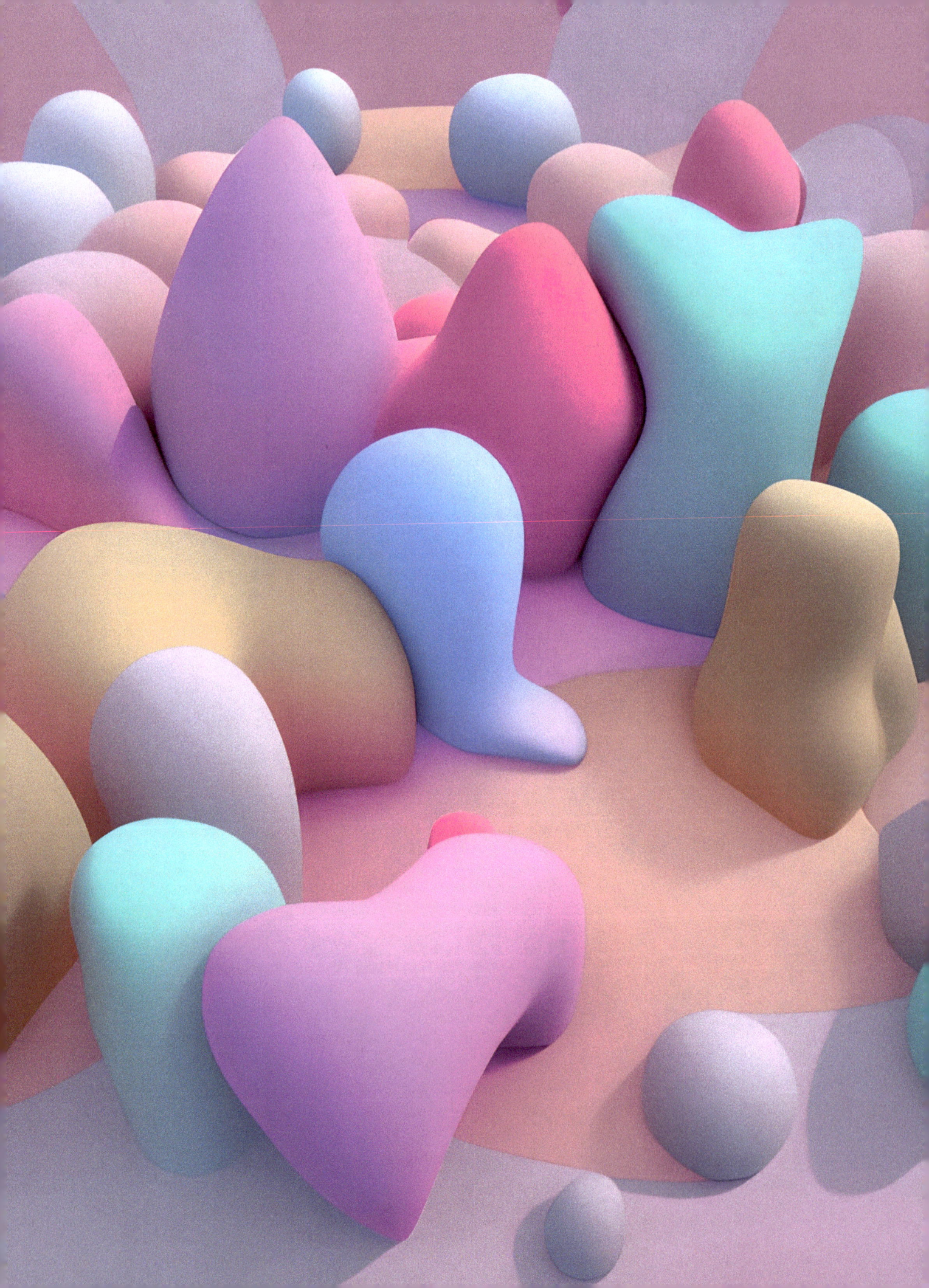

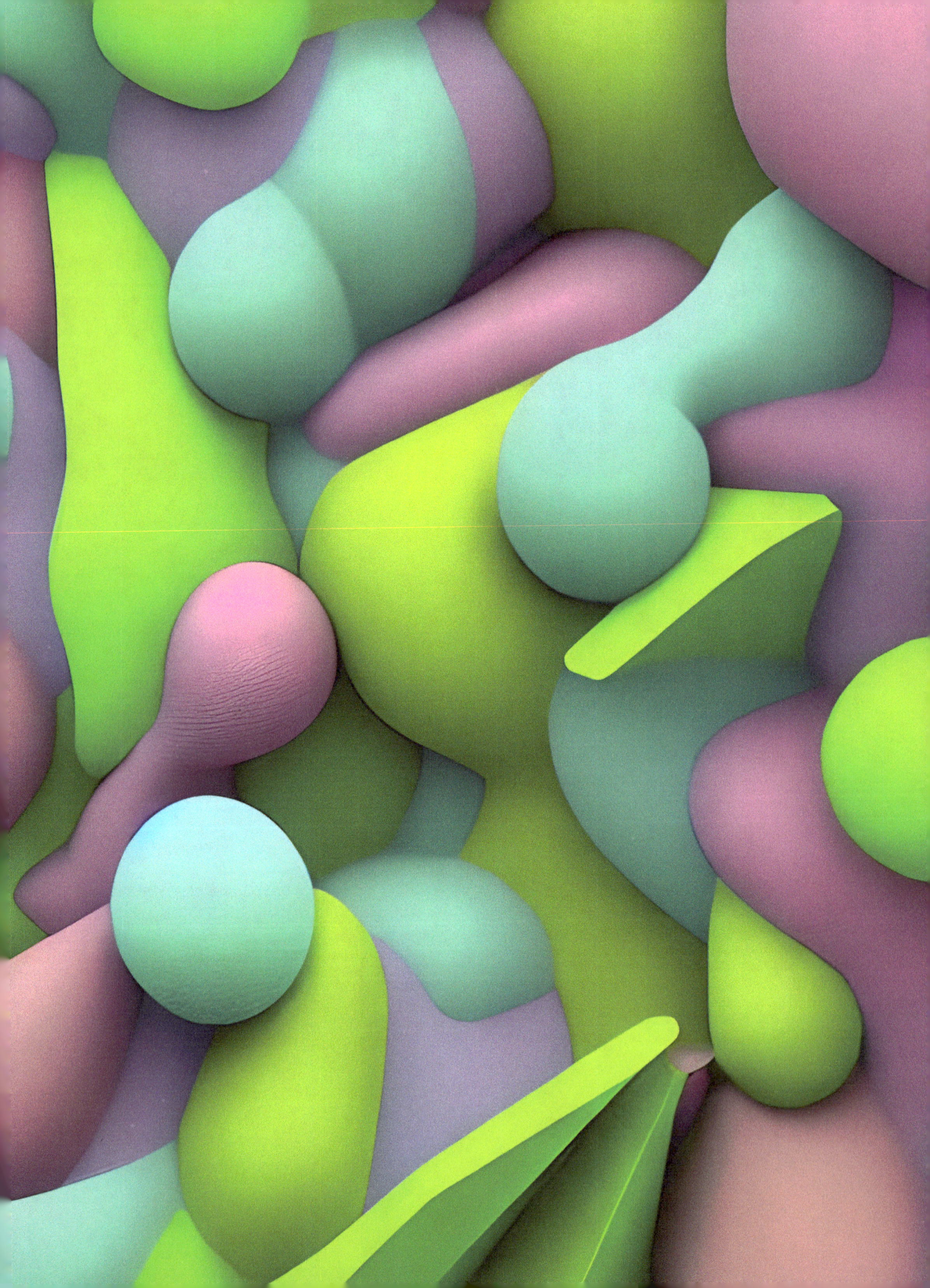

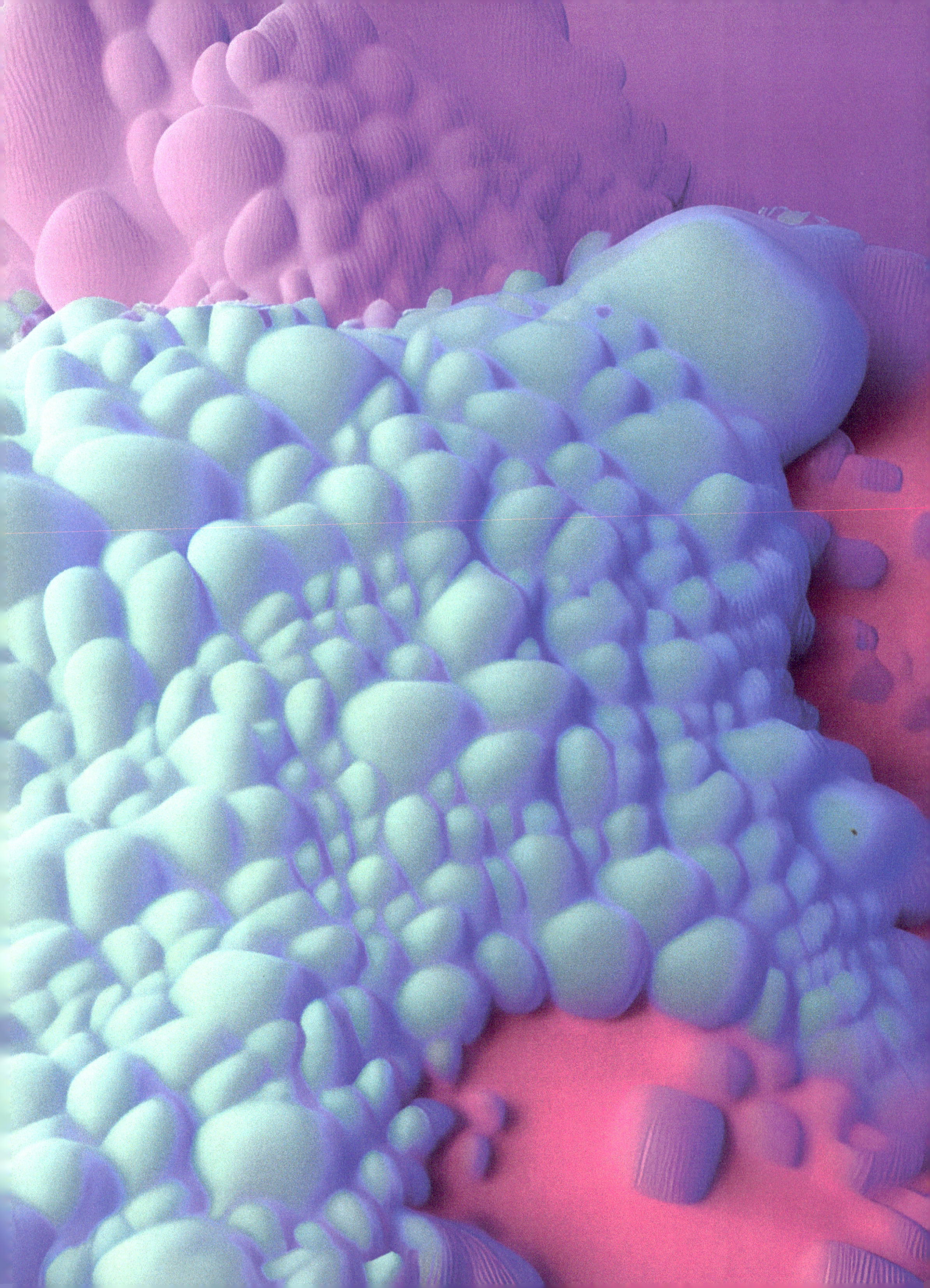

PATTERNS

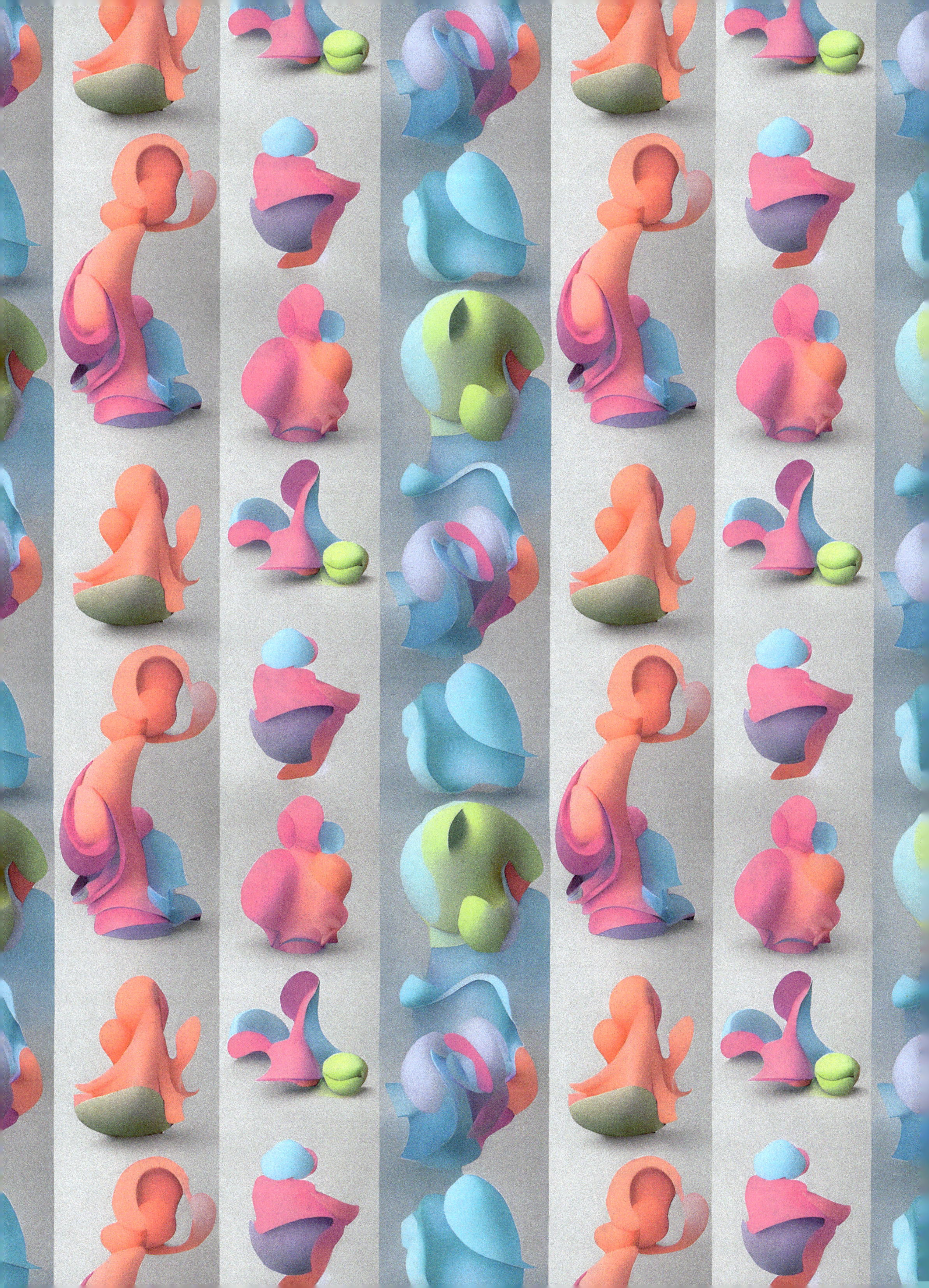

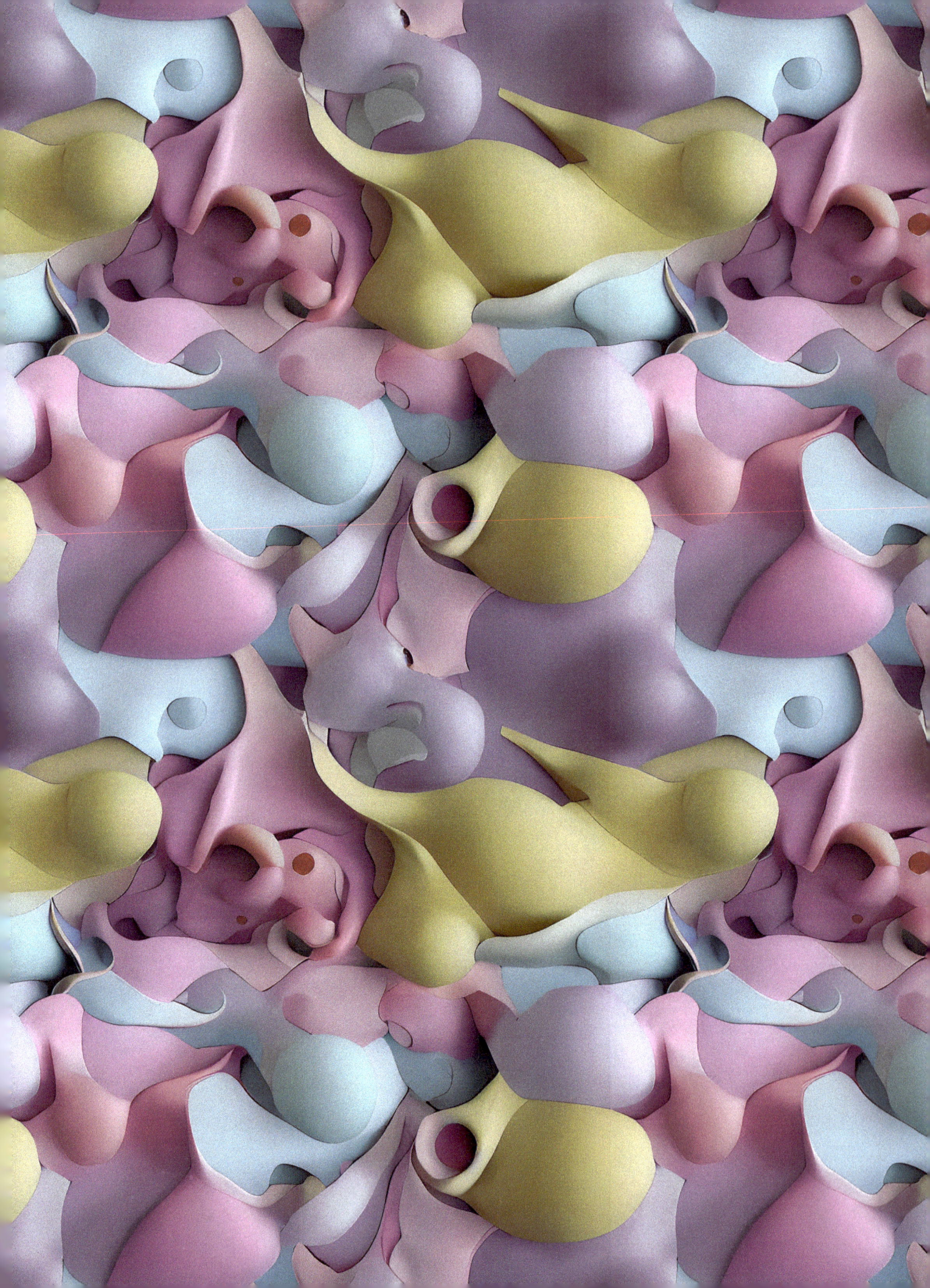

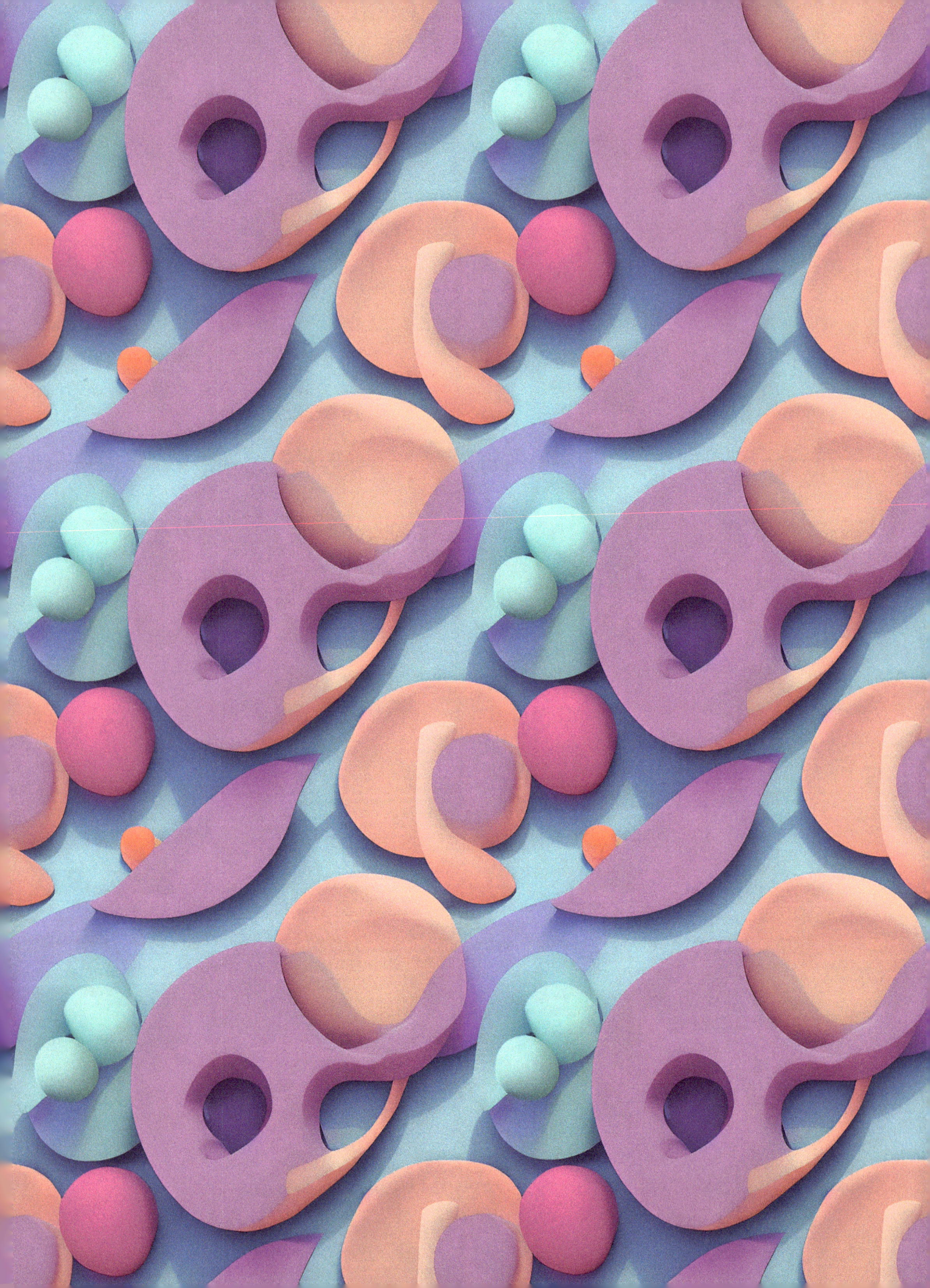

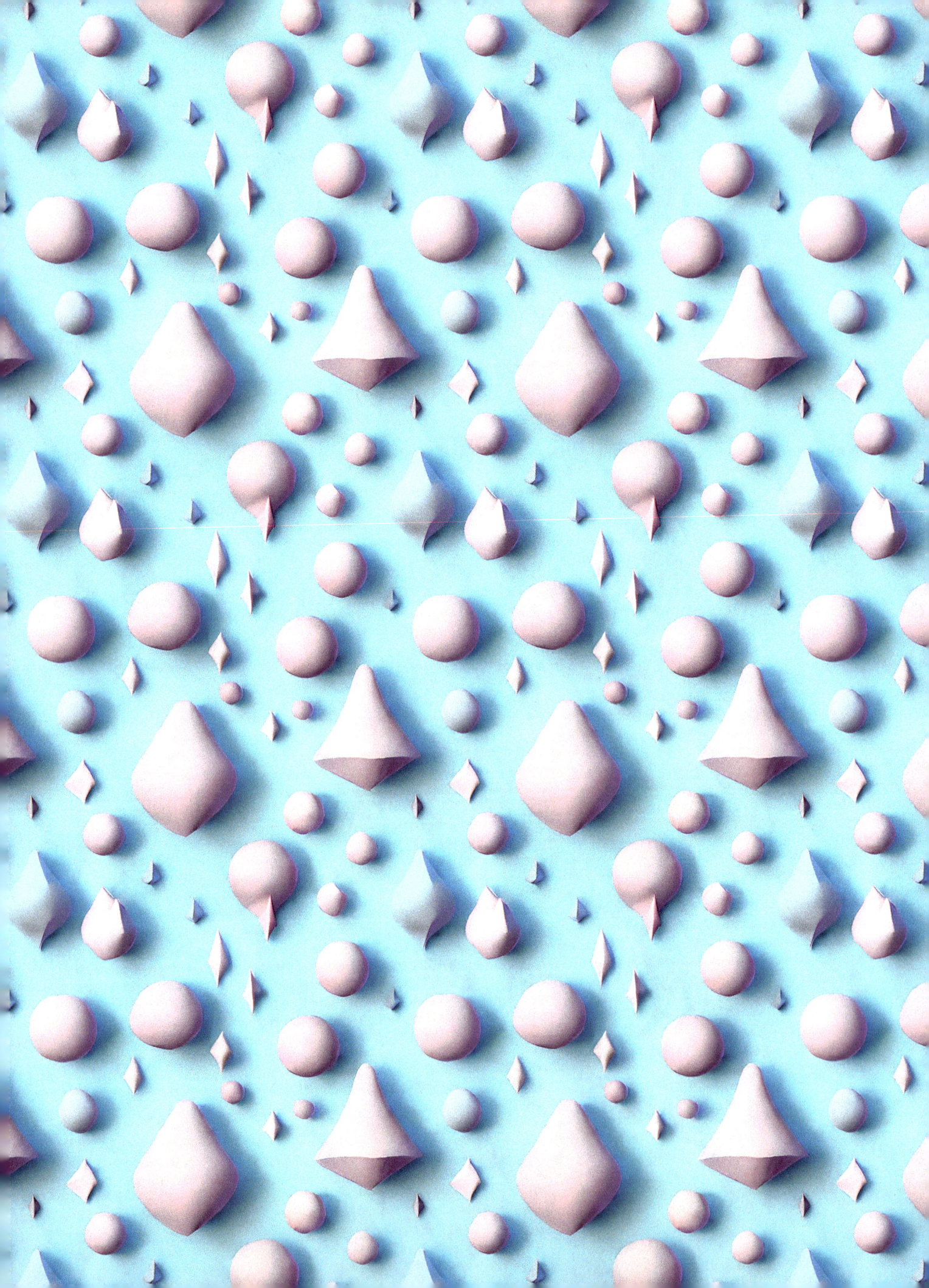

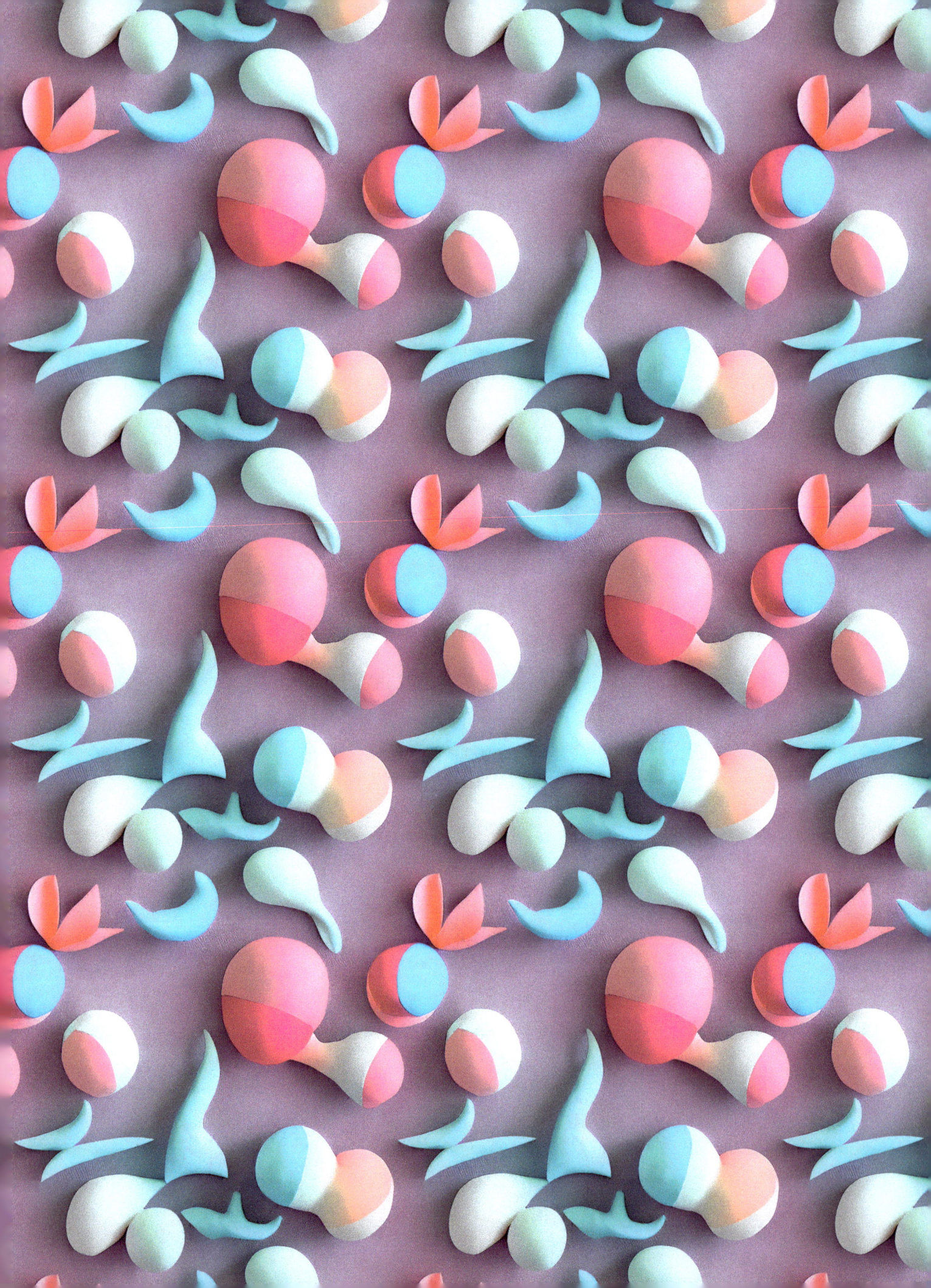

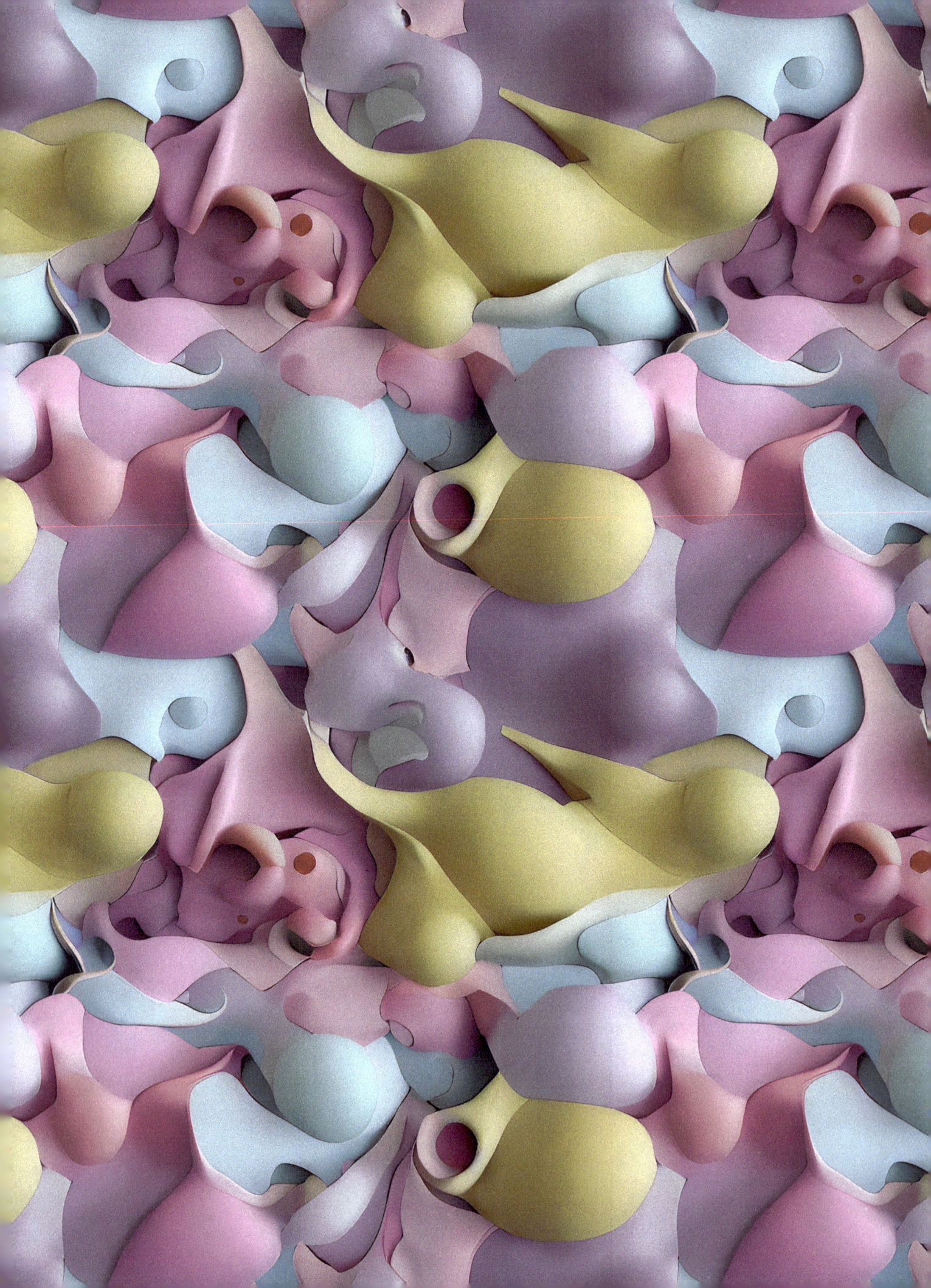

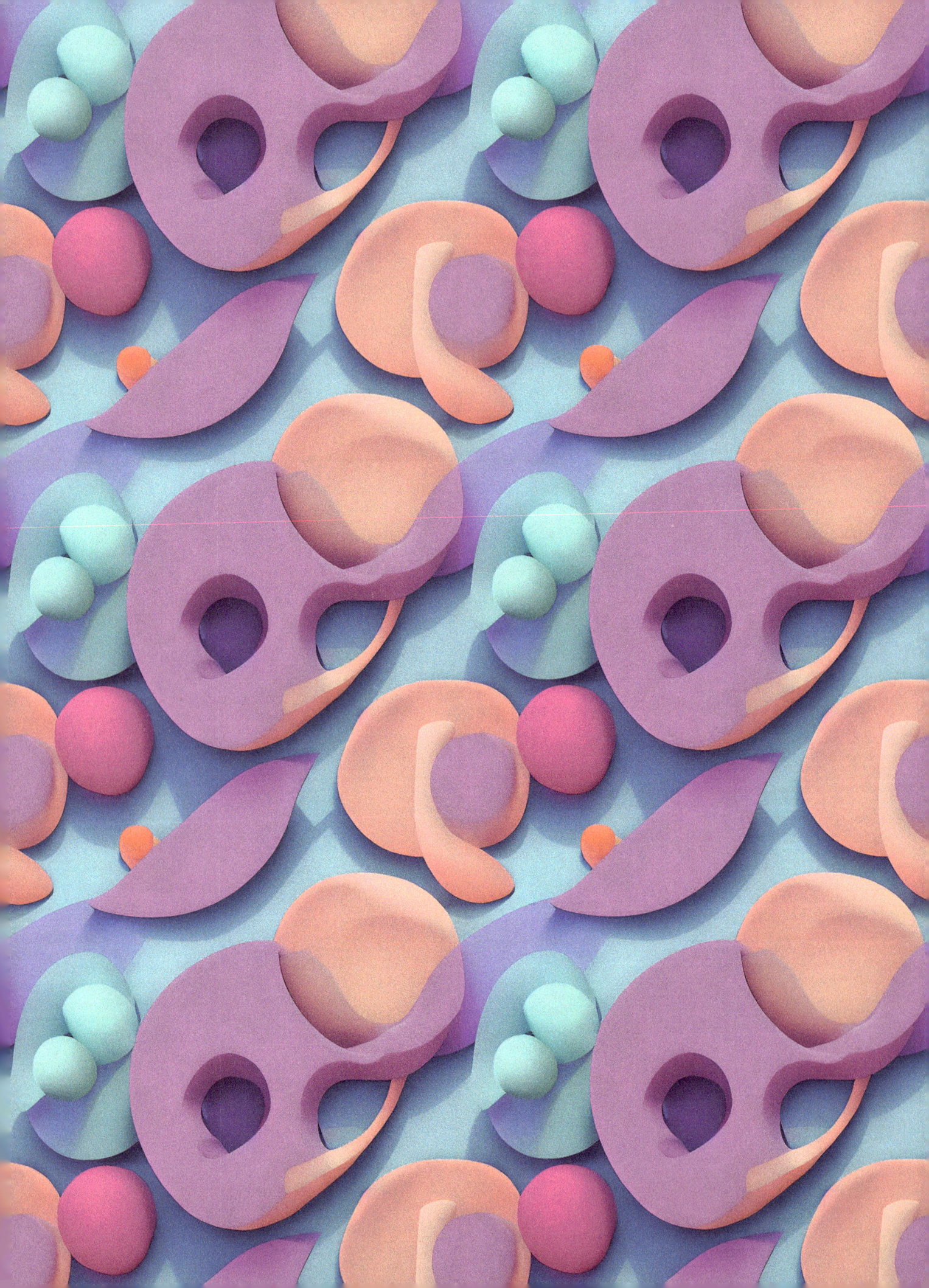

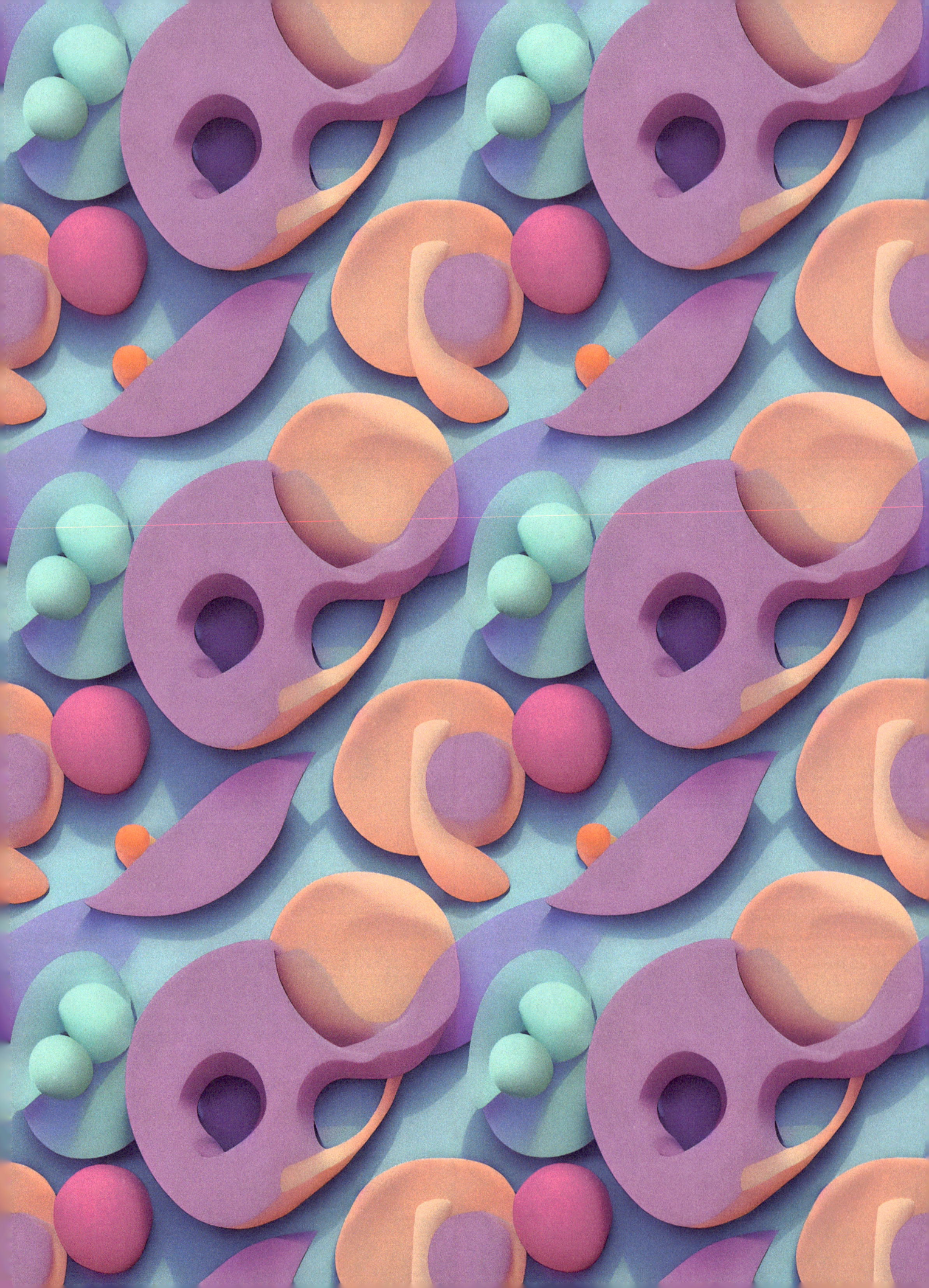

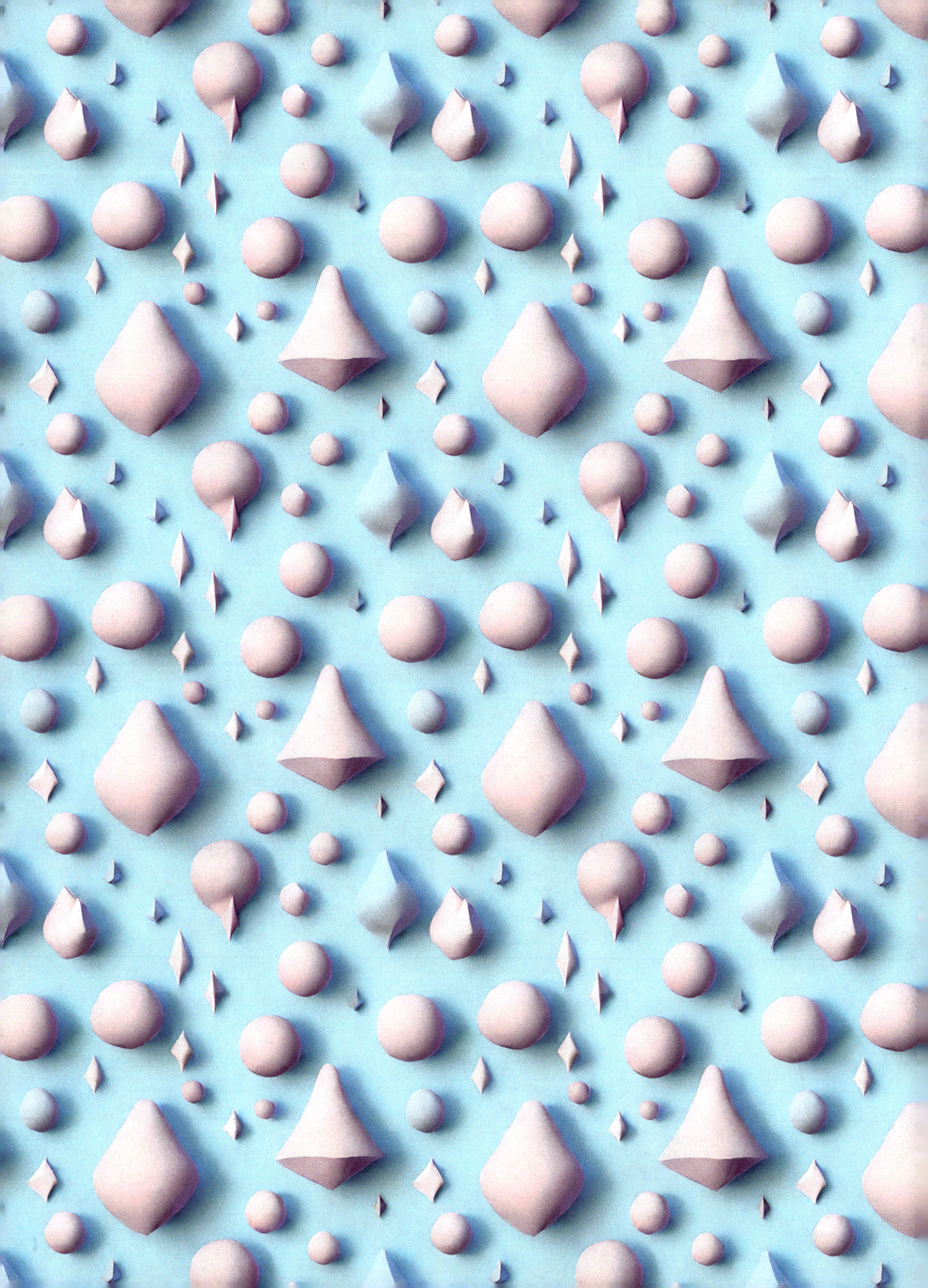

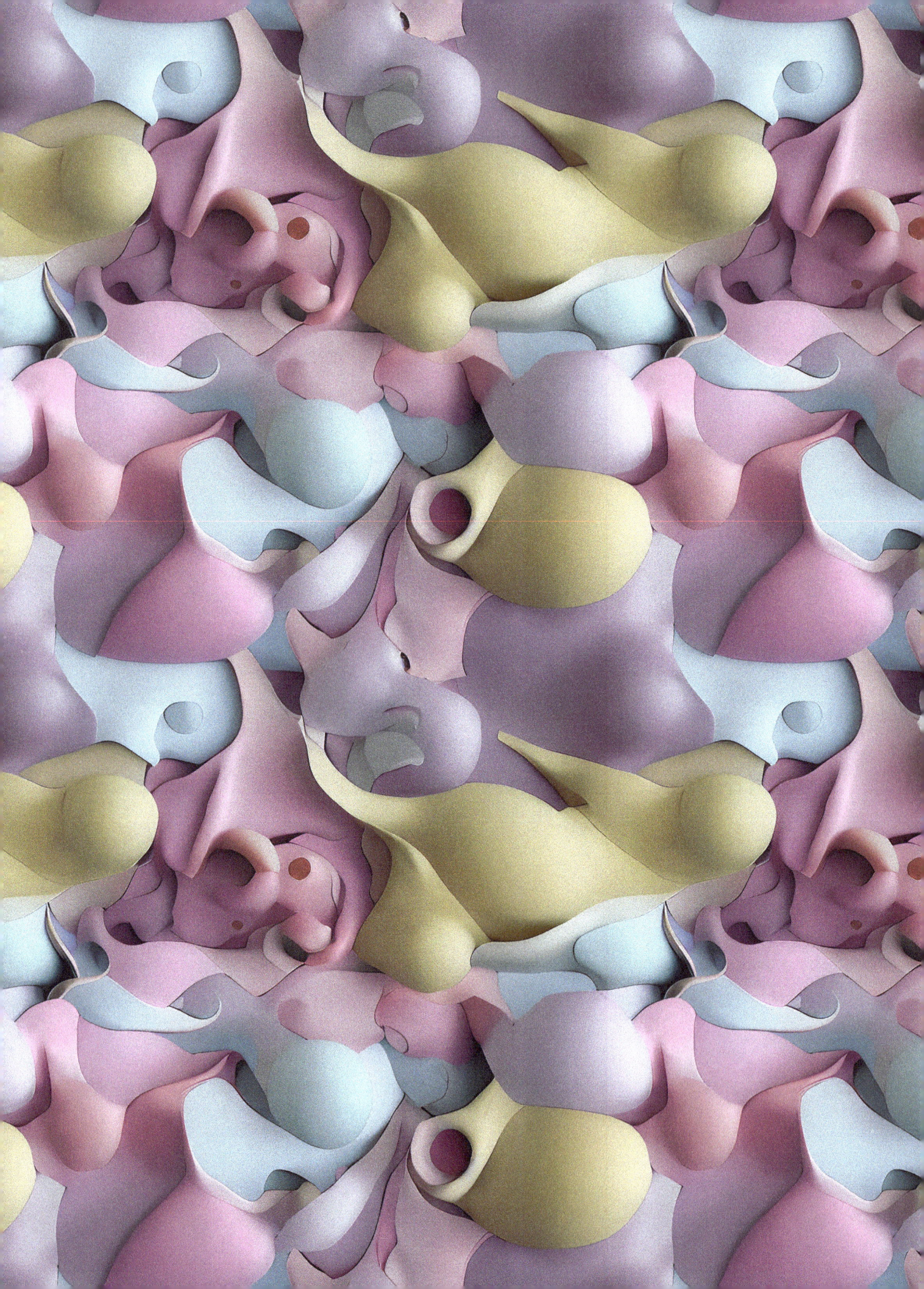

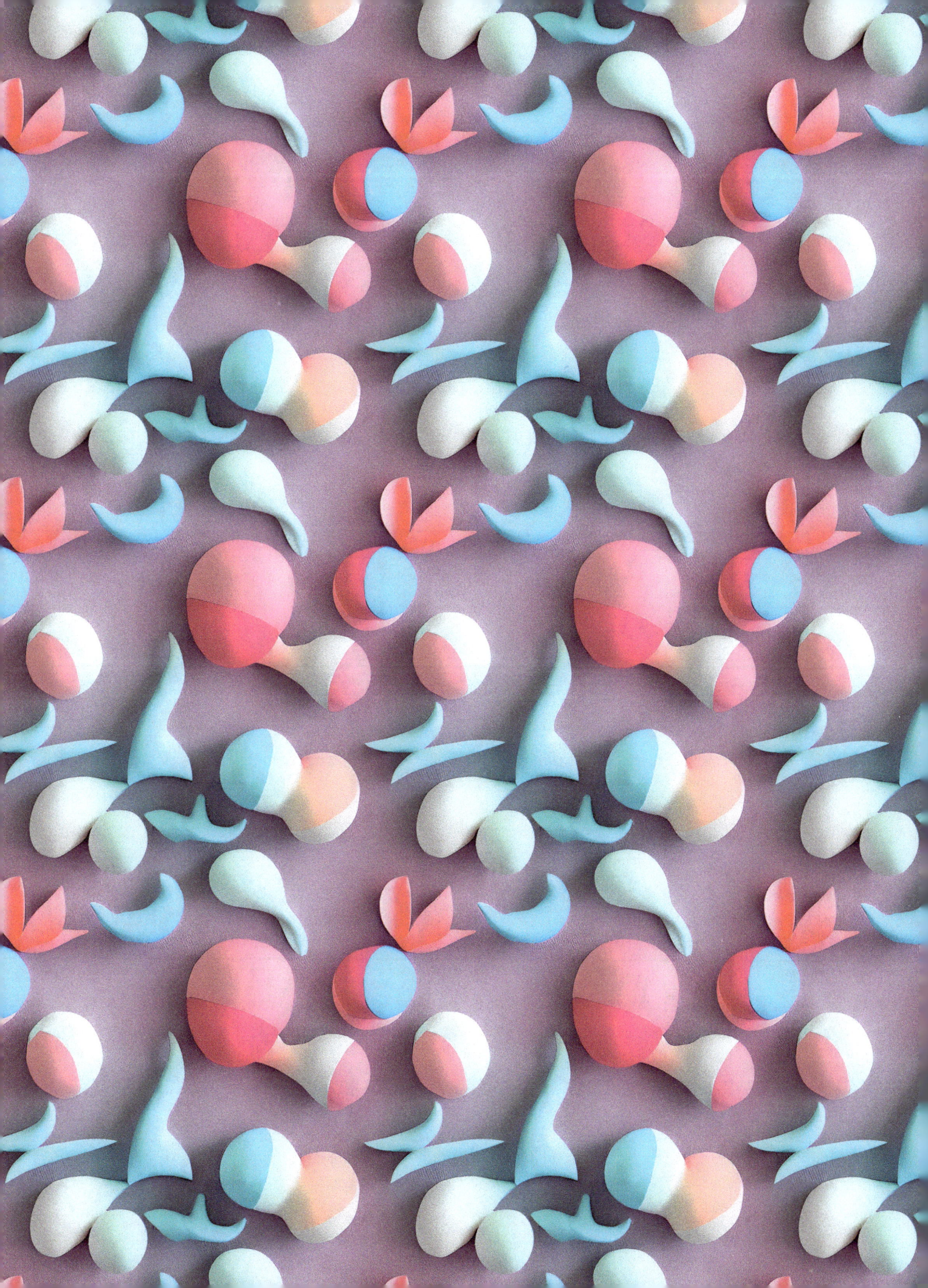

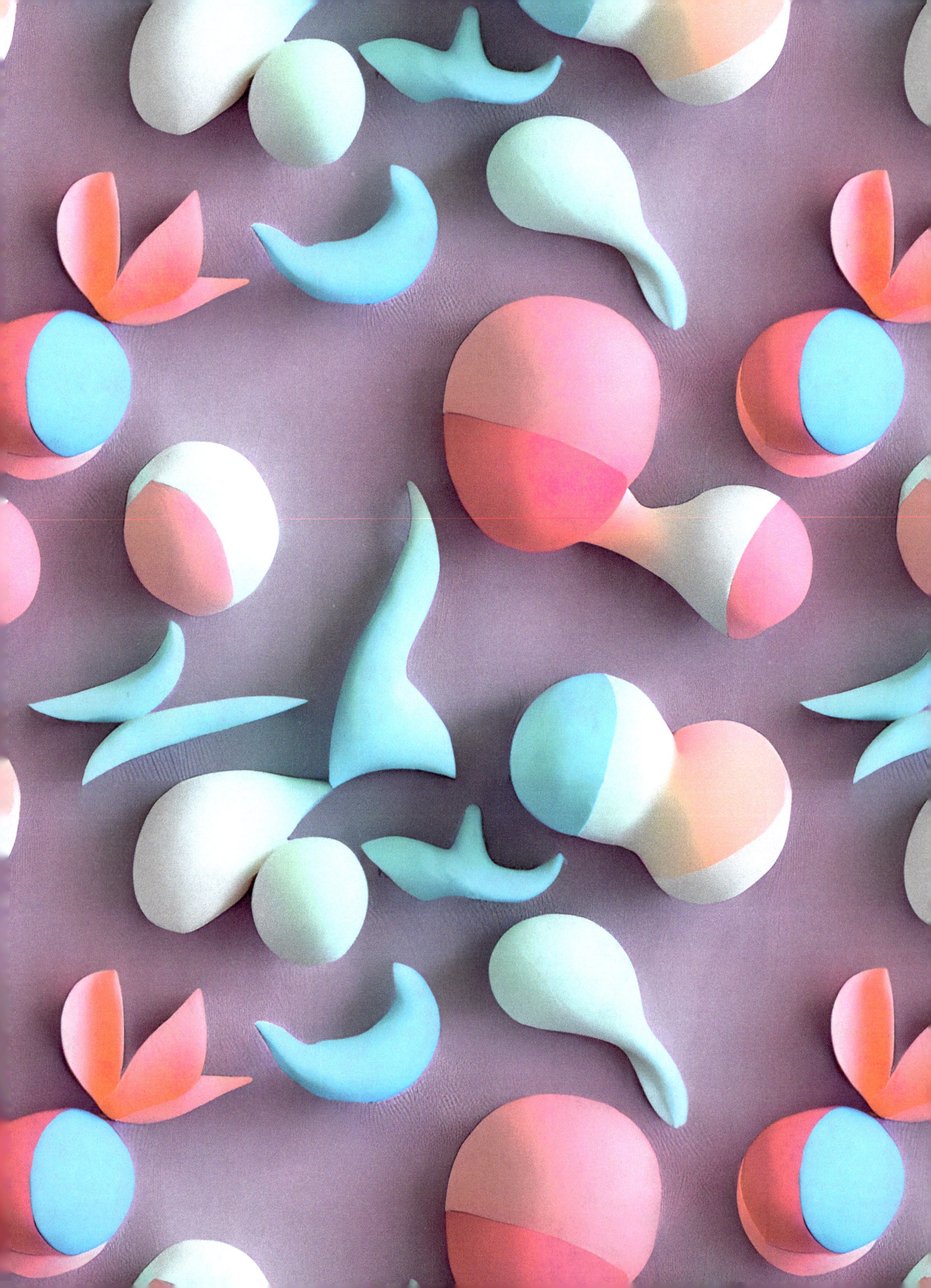

OTHERS IN PRINT AND PATTERN
COLLAGE DECOUPAGE COLLECTION:
-VINATGE SKI ART
-VINATGE UNICORN

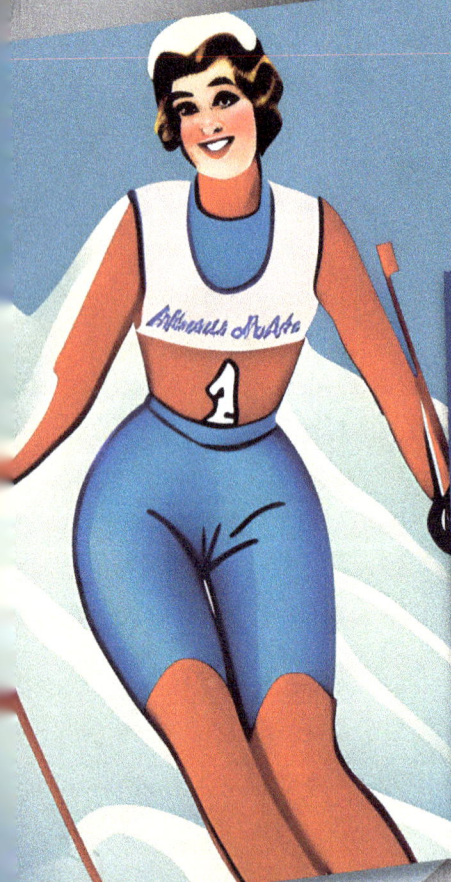

by

sofs

SOFS DESIGNS 2023-24

FIRST EDITION 2023

ISBN 978-1-998930-13-5

CATALOGING DATA AVAILABLE FROM

LIBRARY AND ARCHIVE CANADA

www.ingramcontent.com/pod-product-compliance
Lightning Source LLC
Chambersburg PA
CBHW052113020426
42335CB00021B/2738